HEXHAM
TO
CARLISLE

including the Alston and Brampton Branches

Roger R Darsley

Series editor Vic Mitchell

Roger R. Darsley

MP Middleton Press

Front cover: Class B1 4-6-0 no.61023 **Hirola** *draws across the viaduct into Wetheral station with a train for Carlisle on 16th August 1952. The station retains many of its Newcastle and Carlisle features, in particular the attractive iron and glass awning. The initial absence of platforms is emphasised by the staggered position of the up platform. The pathway across the viaduct to the station can also be seen. This attractive station with its curved platforms is still well maintained today. (J.W.Armstrong Trust)*

Back cover: The South Tynedale Railway's 0-4-0WT Helen Kathryn *waits to return to Alston from its northern terminus at Kirkhaugh in 2005. The locomotive was built by Henschel in 1948. (M.H.Smith)*

Readers of this book may be interested in the following societies:

North Eastern Railway Association,
c/o Mr T Morrell, 8 Prunus Avenue, Kingston Road, Willerby, Hull, HU10 6PH

South Tynedale Railway Preservation Society,
The Railway Station, Alston, Cumbria, CA9 3JB

Published April 2006

ISBN 1 904474 75 6

© Middleton Press, 2006

Design Deborah Esher

Published by
> *Middleton Press*
> *Easebourne Lane*
> *Midhurst, West Sussex*
> *GU29 9AZ*
Tel: 01730 813169
Fax: 01730 812601
Email: info@middletonpress.co.uk
www.middletonpress.co.uk

Printed & bound by Biddles Ltd, Kings Lynn

CONTENTS

INDEX

I. Railways of the area in 1922 with closed stations added.

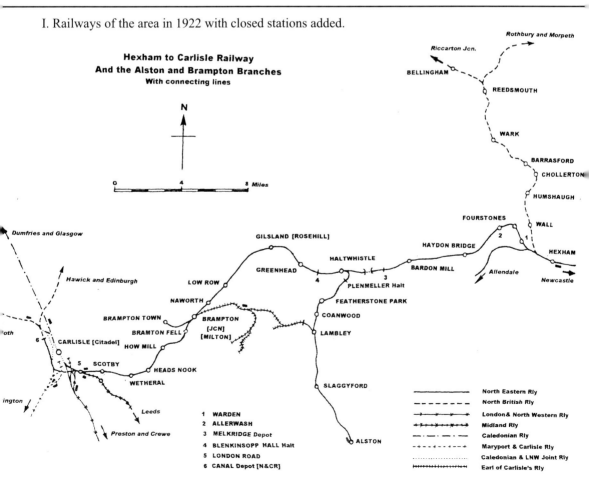

Hexham to Carlisle Railway
And the Alston and Brampton Branches
With connecting lines

ACKNOWLEDGEMENTS

In addition to those acknowledged in the credits, particularly the photographers, I am most grateful to the following people for their assistance in the compilation of this book; V.Mitchell, D.Tyreman for his knowledge and assistance, A.Thompson, D.Charlton and Archivists and Librarians at the Northumberland and Cumbria Record Offices, Newcastle City and Carlisle libraries, and the Tullie Museum, Carlisle, also to my wife, Norma, for the two years when we commuted between Tynemouth and Carlisle.

GEOGRAPHICAL SETTING

Just west of Hexham, the two main tributaries of the River Tyne come together. The Newcastle to Carlisle railway follows the valley of the River South Tyne. At Haltwhistle it leaves the South Tyne and begins to climb over the limestone moors and western elements of the igneous Whin Sill. It crosses the Pennine Fault to drop into the valley of the River Eden and the area of red sandstone. The valleys of the Eden and the River Irthing open out to the broad plain of the Solway Firth and the City of Carlisle, close to the western border with Scotland.

The undulating farmland and deep gorges required heavy engineering with viaducts at Wetheral and Corby. Hell Beck, between Brampton and How Mill has a 73ft high embankment and a 40ft deep cutting. The Cowran Hills cutting is a mile long, with maximum dimensions of 110ft deep and 305ft wide with 14ft high retaining walls. At the time of its construction this was the world's largest cutting.

The Alston Branch climbs the valley of the South Tyne, scaling the tilted plateau of the Alston Block of the Northern Pennines to reach the highest market town in England (1000ft). Haltwhistle, the junction for the branch, is the geographical centre of Great Britain. The branch's most spectacular feature was the number of viaducts, nine in all, of which the most dramatic is the Lambley viaduct and the most architecturally interesting is that at Burnstones over Thinhope Burn.

The Earl of Carlisle's early mineral railway crossed the bare flank of the Tindale Fells to service coal mines in the outcropping lower coal measures. It had outlets at Lambley on the Alston Branch and by rope incline to Milton – later Brampton Junction - and thence to the market town of Brampton, in the valley of the Irthing.

The maps in this volume are scaled at 25ins to 1 mile, unless otherwise stated.

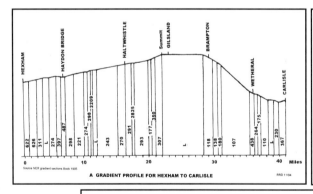

A GRADIENT PROFILE FOR HEXHAM TO CARLISLE

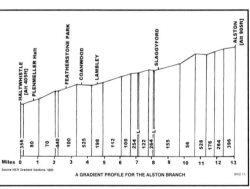

A GRADIENT PROFILE FOR THE ALSTON BRANCH

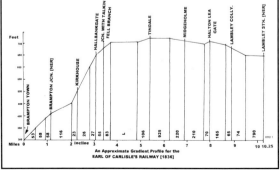

An Approximate Gradient Profile for the
EARL OF CARLISLE'S RAILWAY [1836]

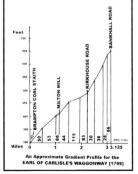

An Approximate Gradient Profile for the
EARL OF CARLISLE'S WAGGONWAY [1799]

HISTORICAL BACKGROUND

Canals between the Tyne and the Solway Firth had been proposed from 1776 but by the time that the Carlisle to Solway Ship Canal was completed in 1823, the idea of a railway, the first to cross the country, albeit at its narrowest point, had gained precedence. The Newcastle on Tyne & Carlisle Railroad Company (NCR) was formed on 26th March 1825. The course of the line was fixed in 1825 and Benjamin Thompson guided the Parliamentary Bill to Assent on 22nd May 1829. Construction began in 1830 simultaneously at Carlisle in the west and Blaydon in the east. The western part of the line from Hexham to Carlisle had most of the major constructions, including the large skew bridge over the River Gelt and the large viaducts at Wetheral and Corby.

The line from Hexham to Haydon Bridge opened on 28th June 1836. Carlisle to Blenkinsopp followed on 19th July 1836 with horse-drawn road coaches meeting the trains to cover the gap. The completed line from Carlisle to Redheugh, Gateshead was opened on 18th June 1838.

The NCR was always an 'eastern' railway with trains down from Newcastle. It was also fairly unusual in that down trains travelled on the right side of the double track. When it was double-tracked throughout, it changed on 7th March 1864 to the more usual left working, though the section from Milton to Carlisle had changed in 1863. Signalling had started with red discs on revolving poles about 1840. These blocked both lines and this is given as an explanation for the number of stations with staggered platforms, as it allowed both platforms to be occupied with the signal turned to red. The gradient and adverse weather problems at the western end of the line led the NCR to be the first railway to fit sanding apparatus and snow ploughs to its locomotives.

The Earl of Carlisle's re-aligned waggonway at Brampton opened on 13th July 1836 and the NCR Carlisle to Blenkinsopp Colliery section opened on the 19th. The NCR lent the Earl the carriage *Emerald* for his opening and he lent the NCR his locomotive, *Gilsland*, for the NCR opening, for, although five locomotives were transported by road from the eastern rail head at Haydon Bridge to Greenhead, only three were ready for use. Four trains left London Road, Carlisle, hauling 48 carriages with 420 passengers. *Gilsland* was not in good condition and the other trains had to wait 45 minutes for it to catch up. *Gilsland* failed on the return journey, but *Hercules* broke a coupling, leaving the Mayor and Corporation of Carlisle stranded for some time until someone noticed – so the honours were about even!

The canal branch at Carlisle was opened on 9th March 1837 and a new station at the Canal Basin replaced a temporary one at Rome Street. The first passenger trains worked through to this station but it was not too convenient for the Carlisle passengers and London Road became the terminus until, under the NER, the NCR managed to get a foothold in the Carlisle Citadel station. Despite allowing the Maryport & Carlisle and the Lancaster & Carlisle Railways use of its London Road station until the Citadel station was built, the NCR was never by itself able to overcome the West Coast railways' stubborn refusal to allow them in.

The NCR eventually joined the North Eastern Railway (NER) on 17th July 1862. In May 1862, the NER negotiated the entry of Newcastle trains into Carlisle Citadel station and this happened from 1864. Warden and Allerwash stations were replaced by Fourstones in 1857. Brampton Fell station closed by 1850 and the private station at Blenkinsopp Hall Halt in 1875. There were few changes then until Naworth closed in 1952. Low Row, How Mill and Scotby closed in 1959. Fourstones, Greenhead, Gilsland, Head Nook and Wetheral all closed on 2nd January 1967 after prolonged debate. Wetheral was reopened on 5th October 1981 following villagers' campaigns.

The Alston branch was surveyed by the NCR at the instigation of the London Lead Company in 1841 but it was 26th August 1846 before the Bill was passed. It took the proposed line through Alston to Nenthead but there was no progress until 1849, when a modified Bill terminated the line at Alston. It included the Lambley Fell branch to connect with the Earl of Carlisle's railway. Construction started in 1850 with the major works being the Lambley and other viaducts. When these were finished, the branch opened its full length on 17th November 1852. The lead industry's decline in this area began in the 1860s and depopulation accompanied it. The branch settled down to be a typical rural branch line. The first serious threat to its existence was in 1959, but closure was rejected because road services could not replace the railway adequately. This was especially so in winter, as the severe winter of 1963 demonstrated. Goods services were closed in 1965 and many economies were made. Despite this, closure was again proposed in 1970. Permission to close the line was given in 1973, subject to improvements to the Haltwhistle-Alston road. Belatedly the beauty of the line's scenery was promoted and many excursion services ran, culminating with 5000 passengers travelling on the last day, Saturday 1st May 1976. In January 1977, the new improved roads were all snow-blocked and the South Tyneside villages cut off! The South Tynedale Railway Preservation Society (STRPS) attempted to buy the line, but the asking price was too high.

Cumbria County Council bought Alston station and the track bed in Cumbria in 1979 allowing STRPS to open a 2ft gauge tourist railway on 30th July 1983. It gradually extended to Kirkhaugh Hall by 1999, with the intention of reaching Slaggyford in the future. Meanwhile the majority of the rest of the trackbed, including the Lambley Viaduct has become an official Northumbrian walking route.

The Earl of Carlisle owned lands on the Tindale Fells where drift-mining of coal had been recorded since the twelfth century. By the 1770s, mining was more organised, but the mines were at a high elevation and transport was a problem. There were established coal roads to Brampton, Alston, Carlisle and Penrith, but cartage was expensive and this kept the cost of coal high. Wooden waggonways were already used within the drifts and the first estimate for a wooden waggonway from Tindale Fell Colliery to Brampton was in 1796. This single-track waggonway was opened on 15th April 1799 and was horse-worked. It served Brampton with coal and limestone at a staith in the town.

In 1819 James Thompson became Lord Carlisle's agent and began both extending the mining and improving the waggonway to a railway. In 1829 he converted the gauge to 4ft 8½in, the same as the NCR, and a horse-drawn 'Dandy' service became available for market days. Thompson was involved in the negotiations for the route of the NCR and, when that was settled, set about in 1835 constructing a new railway which connected Brampton, Kirkhouse, Hallbankgate, Midgeholme and Lambley with a branch to Talkin and Tarnhouse Collieries. There was a rope worked incline (with a gradient of 1 in 17½) between Kirkhouse and Hallbankgate and another at Talkin Colliery. The offices and a wagon repair shop were at Kirkhouse and an engine shed at Hallbankgate. The opening train in July 1836 was from Kirkhouse to Brampton and included the NCR coach *Emerald* with the rest of the 23 'wagons and carriages'. When the Alston branch opened in 1852, the NCR connected with the line at Lambley.

The Dandy wagon worked a regular service from Milton, later renamed Brampton Junction, to Brampton Town. This continued for 45 years until 4th July 1881, when it was replaced by a steam engine, *Dandie Dinmont*, and three coaches. The passenger service was withdrawn on 30th April 1890 and replaced with omnibuses. Continual protests led to the NER signing a 50 year lease with the Countess of Carlisle in 1912. The track and bridge were renewed, a proper station and goods shed built at Brampton Town and the passenger service reopened on 31st July 1913. However, by 1923, all coal to the town was going by road. The NER service was finally terminated on 31st December 1923. Dismantling of the branch took place in September 1924.

The NCR lines, including the Alston branch, became part of the London & North Eastern Railway (LNER) in the 1923 railway grouping and part of British Railways North Eastern Region at nationalisation in 1948.

Despite varying economic fortunes of the mines and the mining companies that leased them, the mineral railway survived to be vested in the National Coal Board (NCB) in 1947. The closure of the last Midgeholme drift meant the end of the railway which was sold for scrap on 31st March 1953 after 155 years of operation. The Lambley West drift continued to use the Lambley Fell Branch until 1958, when it closed and this line was lifted. The line was well known because *Rocket* spent its declining days at work there. It was fitting that the last NCB locomotive to work the line was called *Stephenson*. In the 1980s the NCB Opencast Executive recovered more of the coal reserves in the area, conveying the coal by aerial ropeway to a loading depot at Melkridge near Bardon Mill.

The North Eastern Region was later merged into a larger Eastern Region and upon sectorisation in 1987 passenger services became part of Provincial Railways. This was later renamed Regional Railways. In 1987 Trainload Freight services were to be seen on the line. This became Loadhaul at privatisation in 1994 and was purchased by EWS in 1996. In 2005, EWS, Freightliner and DRS were the freight operators regularly using the route. In 1996 Railtrack took over responsibility for the track. Railtrack was replaced on October 3rd 2004 by the not-for-profit company, Network Rail.

Passenger services were franchised as Regional Railways NE Ltd and the first franchise was taken by Merseyside Transport Ltd (MTL) under the 'Northern Spirit' brand. Arriva bought MTL in 2000 and rebranded the services as Arriva Trains Northern. They lost the franchise on 19th October 2004 to a consortium of Serco and Ned Railways (the UK branch of Nederlandse Spoorwegen). The consortium branded the services 'Northern Rail' and commenced operations on 12th December 2004. In 2005 the Tyne Valley Community Rail Partnership was formed in response to the Government's rural railway policy.

PASSENGER SERVICES

Hexham to Carlisle

In 1854 there were four weekday trains each way to Carlisle and two Sunday services. Despite some opposition, the NCR ran on Sundays from the beginning. The mail train took one hour 32 minutes from Hexham to Carlisle, whereas the 'Parliamentary' trains took one hour 57 minutes, both stopping at all stations. Weekday trains had risen to five by 1880. Most trains stopped at all stations, with limited stop or express trains only really appearing after World War I. In 1890 there were six down trains and seven up trains during weekdays. There was also a down train terminating at Haltwhistle and a later Haltwhistle to Carlisle all station service. From Carlisle, the last train was a 9.40pm to Brampton Junction (on Saturdays it left at 10.00pm). Sunday trains were two each way from Newcastle to Carlisle. All trains took roughly one hour 50 minutes between Hexham and Carlisle.

The 1890s also saw a through Newcastle to Glasgow via Carlisle service with the Caledonian Railway, though this ceased when relations with the North British Railway improved. Another, and longer-lasting, connection was the Ireland boat train and its return (often called the 'Paddy'), which used the Portpatrick and Wigtownshire route to Stranraer. This service still continues, though via Kilmarnock. In 1910 it took one hour 25 minutes non-stop between Carlisle and Newcastle. Semi-fast trains were taking one hour 15 minutes between Hexham and Carlisle, stopping trains took one hour 35 minutes for the same journey. In 1930 there were eight down trains from Newcastle Mondays to Fridays, with two extras on Saturdays. Semi-fast now took one hour 5 minutes and stopping trains one hour 40 minutes. Extra weekday trains included an early morning train from Carlisle to Gilsland and two to Brampton Junction. On Saturdays only there was a late train to Brampton Junction and another to Hexham. From Hexham there were three trains from Newcastle that continued to Haltwhistle and three that started from Haltwhistle back to Newcastle. The Sunday service remained two trains each way from Newcastle to Carlisle, but was augmented by a working from Haydon Bridge.

Economies began to bite after World War II with the closure of the intermediate stations, but the introduction of diesel multiple units in the late 1950s was an improvement for the passenger. In the 1970s there were nine trains each way between Newcastle and Carlisle and two workings each way between Newcastle and Haltwhistle. While classes 101 and 104 brought both economy and some comfort, like the present class 156 units, the same cannot be said for the class 142 four-wheel 'Pacers'. With the integration of the Newcastle-Carlisle line into a network of origins and destinations across the region, it became possible to travel in a 'Pacer' from Saltburn to Barrow-in-Furness via Newcastle, Carlisle and Whitehaven.

In the winter 2004-2005 timetable there are 15 weekday and 11 Sunday Newcastle-Carlisle trains. While Bardon Mill and Brampton have had a reduction in service since the early 1990s, Wetheral was reopened in 1981.

Alston Branch

In 1858 there were two trains each way, 48 minutes being allowed up and down the branch. By 1870 a third train each way had been added and the time allowed reduced to 40 minutes. There was no passenger service on the Langley Fell branch. By 1880 an extra train had been added on Saturday and by 1890 this afternoon extra also ran on Thursday. Reasonable connections were generally provided with east and westbound trains at Haltwhistle. A Sunday service of two trains each way was added in the early 20th century. By mid-1924, the timetable comprised four trains each way on weekdays, one down train being at a different time on Saturdays, but by 1950, the weekday service had increased to six trains each way with an extra late evening train on Saturdays. The Sunday service had ceased. The final timetable was seven down with one Saturdays only and six up with two Saturdays only. From the beginnings of the closure investigations in that year until final closure in 1976 many excursion trains visited the branch.

The South Tynedale Railway tourist services started in 1983 and currently run a seasonal weekend timetable of five trains each way which becomes daily in high season.

1. Hexham to Haltwhistle

HEXHAM

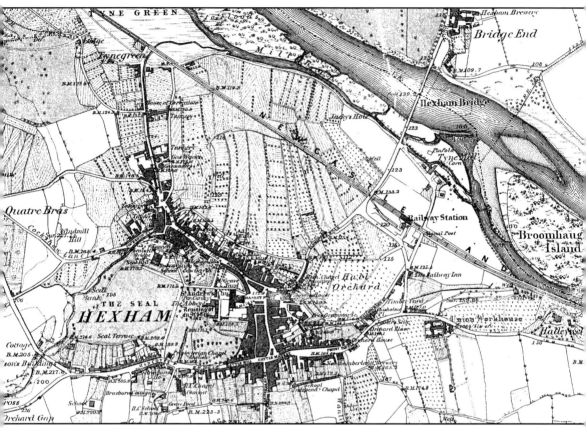

II.   Hexham was, and still is, the most important station between Newcastle and Carlisle. It lies close to the river with the mediaeval town on the hillside to the south as the 1856 six inch to one mile map shows. The station building is at right angles to the line. There is a covered awning over the main lines and two loop lines. Goods facilities are four sidings to the south west and the whole station is protected by a solitary signal post.

(lower left) 1. This engraving by J.W.Carmichael shows the opening of the station in 1835. It has often been published, as in this case, in the form of a postcard by Gibson of Hexham. The locomotive is 0-4-0 no.2 *Comet* which took the second train on opening day. Traffic increased as the town grew (from 7000 in 1901 to 10,000 in the 1960s). The station also grew to have bay platforms, a large goods shed and a two road engine shed. (R.R.Darsley Collection)

2. Hexham was used to unusual military trains going up the Border Counties railway, but this is a class J37 0-6-0 (NBR class S) delivering three new 4-6-0s from Armstrong Whitworth, Elswick, to the London, Midland & Scottish Railway via Carlisle Upperby. The class 5MT 4-6-0s are 5298, 5297, 5296 and the date is late 1936. (B.Greenfield/K.Hoole Collection)

3. No. E56380 and its power car have arrived as the 17.10 from Newcastle on 23rd April 1980. The station continued to handle freight until 1991, though most of the freight facilities were at the east end of the station, where the listed signal box and the goods shed still survive. (T.Heavyside)

4.   The exterior of the station is seen from the west on 17th June 2003. The yard was being upgraded to provide a bus interchange and a lit carpark. The original trainshed was replaced in 1871 by conventional platforms with glazed awnings and end screens. The station buildings were also enlarged to give more accommodation, as it became the junction for the lines to Allendale and to Hawick. (R.R.Darsley)

5.   The down platform with the main station buildings has a wide glazed canopy supported by a double row of columns. In 2005 the station was still staffed and had a continued tradition of magnificent floral displays. In 2005, Hexham won the 'station of the year' category in the National Rail Awards. (R.R.Darsley)

Other photographs and a more detailed map can be found in the companion album, **Newcastle to Hexham.**

WEST OF HEXHAM

6.　　This view of Border Counties Junction shows the points set to cross the bridge so that class J21 0-6-0 no.65103 on the 1955 "Gardens Special" can continue to Bellingham. The signal box arches over the double track line to Carlisle. (R.F.Payne/J.W.Armstrong Trust)

III.　　The original wooden bridge at Warden burnt down in 1848. It was rebuilt in cast iron on the original piers. The 1899 map shows this bridge and superimposed, by the original map owner, are pencil lines showing the alignment of the new bridge built in 1903. Today the bases of the old bridge are still visible downstream.

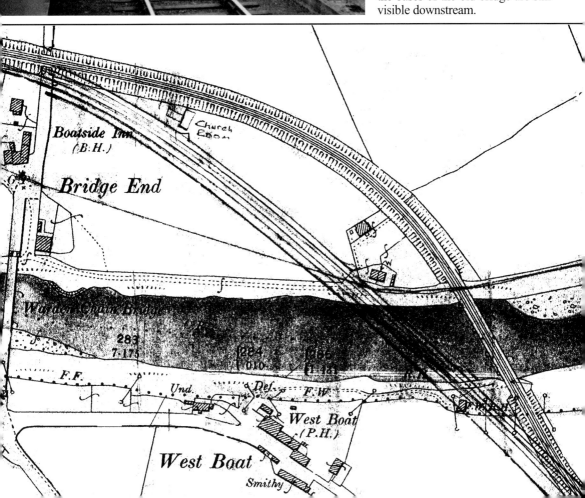

WARDEN

7.   The station was closed in 1837 when it and Allerwash were replaced by Fourstones. NCR stations did not originally have platforms and this heavily rebuilt cottage is likely to have been the ticket office. The village is beyond the road bridge. (R.R.Darsley)

8.   To the west of Warden is the South Tyne Paper Mill which was rail connected. Here Co-CoDE no.60083 with an empty limestone train to Hardendale, Shap, crosses the road by the mill on its way to Carlisle on 30th June 2003. (R.R.Darsley)

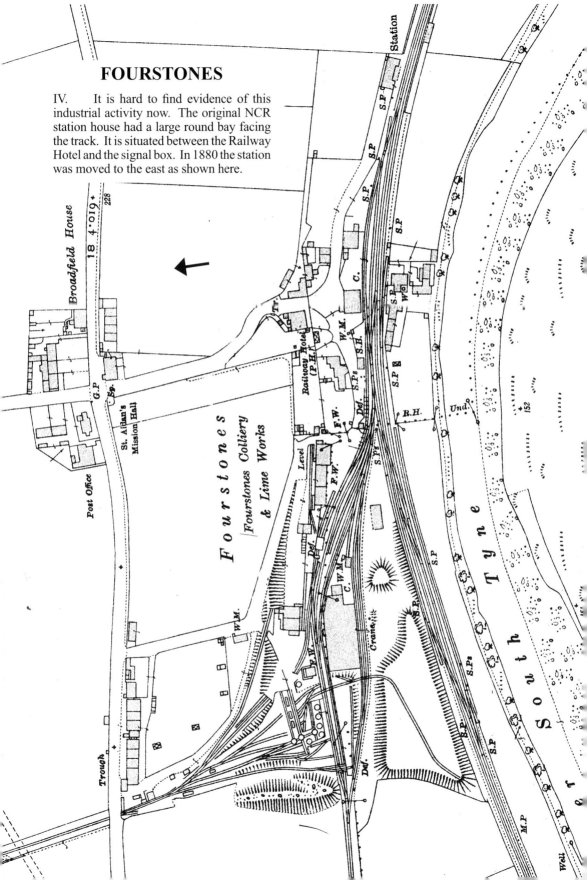

FOURSTONES

IV. It is hard to find evidence of this industrial activity now. The original NCR station house had a large round bay facing the track. It is situated between the Railway Hotel and the signal box. In 1880 the station was moved to the east as shown here.

9.   The original single-storey stone station house is now a private house. This 1880 station was built in the NER twin pavilion style. The shunting signals are NER slotted signals. The down platform was reached by the wooden barrow way. (Beamish Museum)

10.   This view is from the down platform after closure to passengers on 2nd January 1967. Goods traffic ceased on 26th April 1965 but the track to the goods yard is still in place though the wooden goods shed is in tatters. The stone shed behind this skeleton structure is still in use as garages. (K.Hoole Collection)

11.   To the north of the station area was the large Fourstones Colliery and Lime Works. Besides standard gauge sidings, William Benson & Son Ltd operated a narrow gauge railway system in the quarries. It had the unusual gauge of 3ft 1½ in. This is their first loco, built by Black Hawthorn as no.1082 in 1893. The railway was closed in 1942 and the locos scrapped by 1945. (Beamish Museum)

ALLERWASH

12.   This station closed in 1837, but the three cottages survive, one of which must have been a ticket office. They are now one private residence. The footpath to the down line passes under the railway and is the photographer's vantage point in February 2005. (R.R.Darsley)

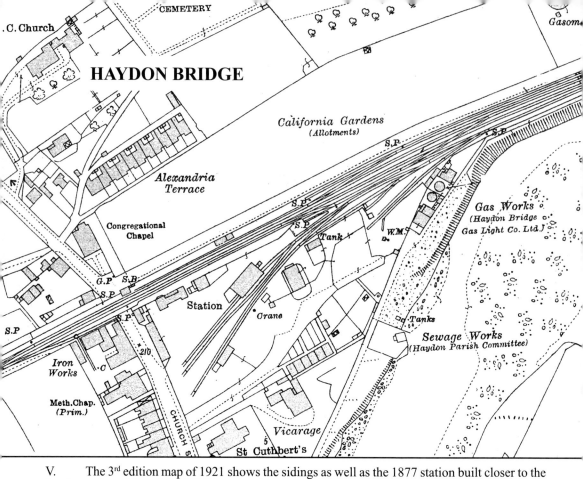

V.   The 3rd edition map of 1921 shows the sidings as well as the 1877 station built closer to the level crossing. The original NCR station building is found between the tank and the 5-ton crane.

13.   The NCR station was a temporary terminus to the line from 1836-8 and the station building with its triple-arched porch is very pleasant. The development of the railway left this building in the goods yard where it survived until 1965. (K.Hoole Collection)

14.   The 1877 buildings gave the station a rather grim appearance. There was no footbridge and the NCR simple open shelter remained on the up platform. The house remains, but the waiting rooms and offices were replaced with relatively attractive 'bus shelters' in 1989. (Beamish Museum)

15.   The signal box was at the west end of the platforms. Here interest is centred on the arrival of class K1 2-6-0 no.2005 and class 5MT 4-6-0 no.4767 double heading a Middlesbrough to Hellifield excursion on 24th October 1981. (T.Heavyside)

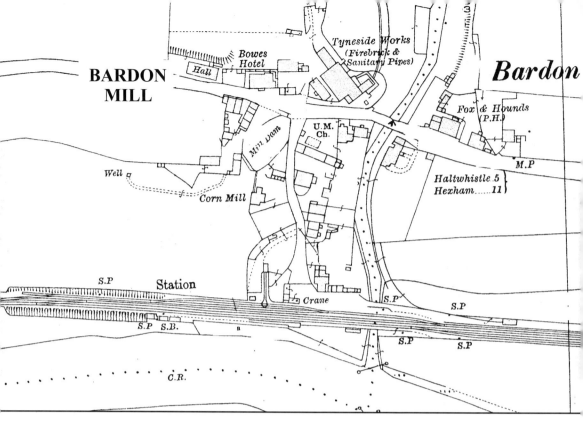

VI. The 1921 map appears confusing, as the label 'station' is some way to the west of the buildings, which are to the north of the label 'crane'. The down platform faces them and the up platform is some 50 yards to the east. The wagon turntable appears to lead to a coal drop.

16. Bardon Mill is an attractive village and the station is down a lane from the village square. This scene is the approach to the station in 1900. The tall triple chimney marks the NCR station house, now a private dwelling. The platforms were built later than the house and the down platform can be seen opposite it. (Newcastle City Libraries)

17.   These are the station house and the station buildings in 1900. A locomotive is shunting a pick-up freight train in the goods yard. Passengers to Hexham and Newcastle must walk between the fences to the platform. (Newcastle City Libraries)

18.   In 1967, the station buildings were in good repair, as they still are today. The goods facilities and dock have become derelict though wagon load freight appears to be accepted. General freight had ceased on 26th April 1965. The up platform and its shelter can be seen in the distance. Crossing the line was by a wooden barrow way and the signal box was to the west of the down platform behind the photographer. (Stations UK)

19.　　A closer view of the up platform shows that the building is a heavily modified NCR open platform shelter. The platform lighting was still gas. (K.Hoole Collection)

20.　　There was some amusement at Bardon Mill on 24th July 1985, when Co-CoDE no.37093 in police livery with a roof light flashing, heads east on the down line chasing Bo-BoDE no.43078 and no.43093 travelling on the up line. Needless to say, it was for a TV advert. (I.S.Carr)

21.　　In 1982, the down platform was demolished and a new timber platform built opposite the up platform thus making passengers in both directions walk the extra 50 yards! Electric light also came at the same time. A new waiting shelter and flower tubs were present in June 2003. (R.R.Darsley)

WEST OF BARDON

22.   Bardon Mill Colliery, north of the station, was a drift mine, originally shunted by an electric hauler and a rope, but output increased and from 1954 a locomotive was used. Here NCB 0-4-0ST no.40 (Barclay no.2280 of 1950) shunts on 26th August 1970. Much of the coal went to Carlisle power station, but the colliery closed in November 1973. (I.S.Carr)

23. Melkridge was a recent coal loading site for Plenmeller open cast colliery. The coal came by conveyor to a hopper house and discharge point. Co-CoDE no.56048 is loading coal for export at Tyne Coal Terminal on 28th March 1996. The site closed and was cleared in 2000 though the siding remains and is still signalled. (P.J.Robinson)

24. Class V2 2-6-2 no.60809 *The Snapper, The East Yorkshire Regiment, The Duke of York's Own* is leaving the western portal of Whitchester tunnel on 16th May 1959. Due to land slippage most of the ornamental stonework has been removed and the entrance is now heavily braced with steel girders. (R.Leslie)

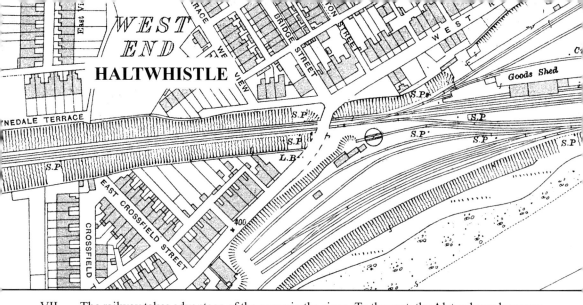

VII.   The railway takes advantage of the curve in the river. To the east, the Alston branch curves south to its river crossing. To the west, goods sidings and the turntable are fitted in before the West Road overbridge.

25.   Haltwhistle is an important station, because of the site of the town, which proudly boasts that it is the geographical centre of Britain. The name has no railway origins being either 'Alt Wessel' or 'Haut Twysell'. It was the junction for the Alston branch and the branch DMU waits for the starter signal. (Beamish Museum)

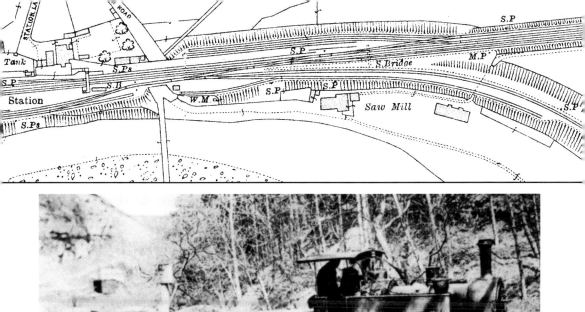

26.　　At the east of the town, Town Foot, was a sharply curved siding to the interchange with the Cawfield Whinstone Quarry narrow gauge line. The Newcastle Granite & Whinstone Co. Ltd. opened the quarry in 1902 and it ran parallel to the South Tyne Colliery system which also used this interchange. This is the 2ft gauge 0-4-0T *Vyrnwy* Kerr Stuart no.748 of 1902. The system was replaced by road transport in 1935. (Beamish Museum)

27.　　A panorama of Haltwhistle station from the west in 1893 shows the facilities of the station: a large goods station, cattle docks, and a turntable. On the right is the South Tyne River and in the background the viaduct for the Alston Branch. The branch train is in the island platform. (Newcastle City Libraries)

28.	Photographed under the waist of the signal box, the class G5 0-4-4T has the signal to enter the branch platform. A Newcastle train has stopped at the up platform. Almost totally screened by the bunker of the G5 is a down train with a class B1 or K1 loco just arriving and in the line that was originally the Town Foot siding is a K1 2-6-0 on a freight train. Haltwhistle was rarely this busy! (K.Hoole Collection)

29.	Class B1 4-6-0 no. 61014 *Oribi* arrives at Haltwhistle on 12th April 1952. The station buildings are on the left fenced off from the track. The up platform is hidden by the arriving train. The single-storey building with the clock is now the Tourist Office and the other buildings are private premises in good repair. (J.W.Armstrong Trust)

30.	It is December 1960 and a DMU gives the passenger a forward view of the starting signal and of class K1 2-6-0 no. 62050 passing on a freight train, while the Alston DMU waits to enter the station. (R.R.Darsley)

31. The 15.30 DMU from Newcastle is crossing over to return to Hexham on 26th August 1970. The siding to the goods shed has been removed, goods traffic having long ceased. The down platform is the north face of the Alston branch island platform. (I.S.Carr)

→

32. No.142094 arrives on 30th June 2003. Under the NER footbridge is the up platform. Built in 1901 the signal box is a listed building and its restoration won a National Railway Heritage Award in 2003. (R.R.Darsley)

→

33. Haltwhistle has also a water tank, built in 1861. Peter Tate was the engineer and H Wylie & Co, the fabricator. It has been restored as an office. In front of the signpost is a display panel with the history of the station. Behind are a set of cycle lock-ups in this June 2003 view. (R.R.Darsley)

2. Alston Branch

34.   The Alston branch was locally much appreciated in a bad winter, though that did not prevent some caustic complaints about its speed and efficiency. (Beamish Museum)

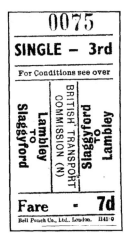

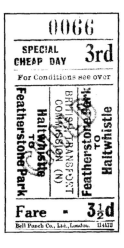

HALTWHISTLE

35.   The branch line had its own platform at Haltwhistle, the south face of the island platform. BR standard class 3MT 2-6-0 no.77014 awaits passengers for the 11.50 on Saturday 30th March 1957 (I.S.Carr)

36.   Class J39 0-6-0 no.64853 crosses the River South Tyne viaduct and climbs out of Haltwhistle with the 17.40 to Alston on 22nd June 1957. The branch closed in 1972 but the viaduct is still a landmark on the A69. (R.Leslie)

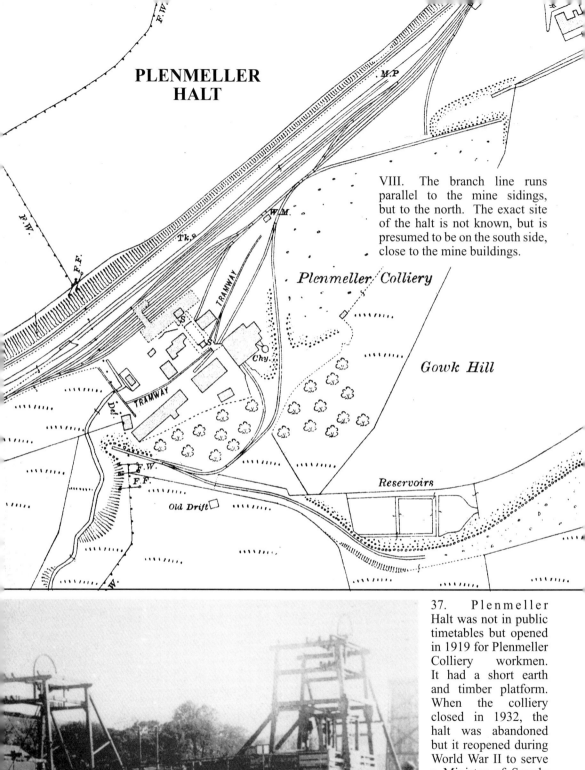

PLENMELLER HALT

VIII. The branch line runs parallel to the mine sidings, but to the north. The exact site of the halt is not known, but is presumed to be on the south side, close to the mine buildings.

Plenmeller Colliery

Gowk Hill

Reservoirs

Old Drift

37. Plenmeller Halt was not in public timetables but opened in 1919 for Plenmeller Colliery workmen. It had a short earth and timber platform. When the colliery closed in 1932, the halt was abandoned but it reopened during World War II to serve a Ministry of Supply depot until 1946. (Beamish Museum)

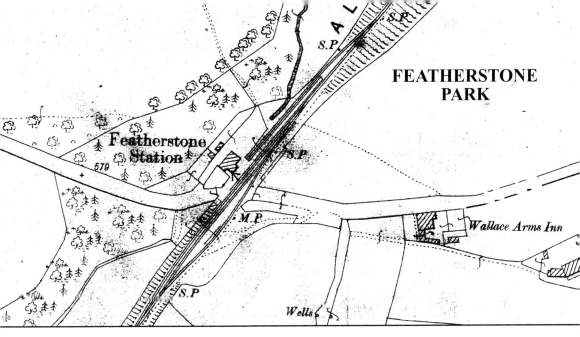

FEATHERSTONE PARK

IX. The 2nd edition 1900 map shows a simple but sufficient layout for the station. The absence of a village close by suggests that business was never going to be very brisk.

38. Opened in 1852 as Featherstone, the station became Featherstone Park in 1902 and Featherstone Park Halt from 1933 to 1937. The station was unmanned from 1954, when goods traffic ceased. The stone-built station house is now a private residence. The oil lamp had another variation on the station name 'Featherston Park'. The goods bay has been removed. (Stations UK)

39. The platform had several levels as can be seen in this photograph. The signal box has gone. After the branch's reprieve in 1963, the station became one of the first to have black and white name-boards in the then new 'corporate identity'. (Stations UK)

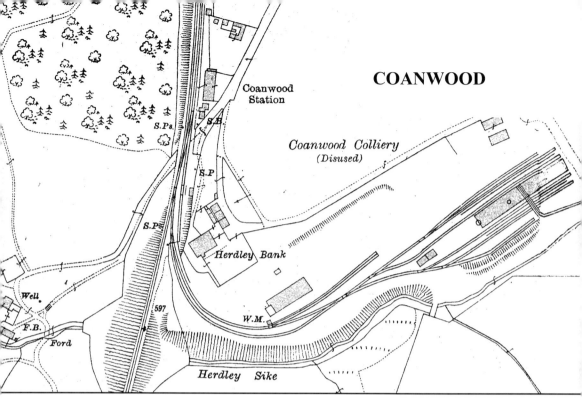

COANWOOD

X. The station layout is minimal, as all shunting could be done in Coanwood colliery sidings. The site also took coal from East Coanwood colliery. This was bought by a narrow gauge railway of about a mile long, which ended over the coal bunkers at right angles to the sidings.

40. Coanwood had several existences. As Shaft Hill, it was a temporary southern terminus but closed in 1853. It reopened as Shafthill in 1863 and changed its name to Coanwood in 1885. Coanwood colliery closed around 1920, but East Coanwood colliery (also known as Crystalwell) survived until 1944. (K.Hoole Collection)

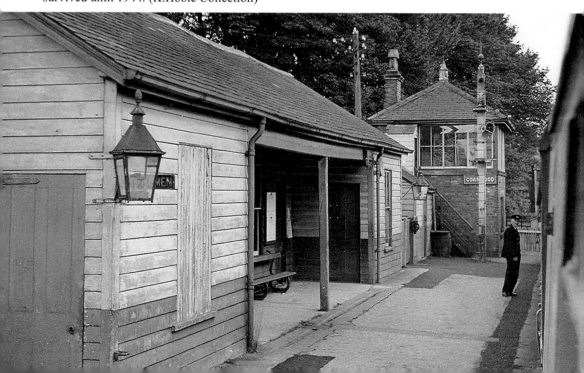

41.   In 1967, the large waiting shed and office and the signal box have disappeared, but the smaller shed has been painted and there is a new fence and a BR black and white nameboard. (Stations UK)

42.   A regular way of working was for the freight train locomotive to come up with the passenger train and to pick up freight on the way back. Here class J21 0-6-0 no.5101 and class G5 0-4-4T no.7277 are on their way to Alston. (E.E.Smith/R.R.Darsley Collection)

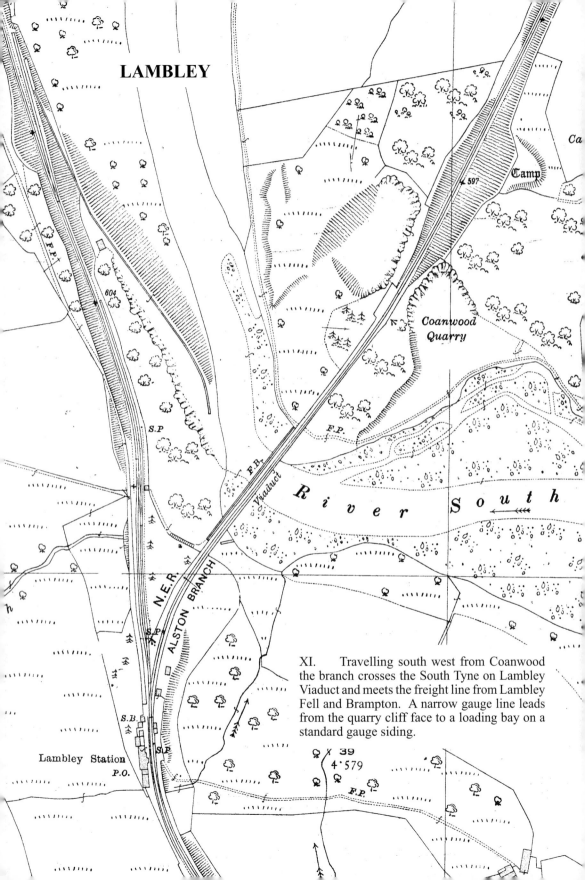

LAMBLEY

Coanwood Quarry

Camp

River South

XI.   Travelling south west from Coanwood
the branch crosses the South Tyne on Lambley
Viaduct and meets the freight line from Lambley
Fell and Brampton. A narrow gauge line leads
from the quarry cliff face to a loading bay on a
standard gauge siding.

Lambley Station
P.O.

N.E.R.

ALSTON BRANCH

Viaduct

S.P

S.B.

F.P.

F.B.

F.P.

F.P.

804

597

39
4·579

43. This favourite vantage point shows the viaduct, the station and the colliery sidings. Class J39 0-6-0 no.64814 leaves with the 11.56 Haltwhistle to Alston train one day in November 1956. (J.W.Armstrong Trust)

44. Lambley Viaduct is 110ft above the river with nine arches of 58 feet, seven of 20 feet and two of 12 feet. It is more dramatic than the other listed viaduct at Thinhope Burn which is technically interesting but less photogenic. After the branch line had been reprieved, it became popular with excursion trains such as this train of two 4-car class 101 DMUs. (I.S.Carr)

45.   The station was in a cramped site at the south end of the viaduct. Behind is the junction with the line to Lambley Colliery and a class J39 0-6-0 is shunting the coal sidings. The path to the station comes down past the signal box. The lower platform was the original, the later addition was higher. (K.Hoole Collection)

46. The diesel multiple unit blocks the fine view of the viaduct from the station. The original station has a central gable. In the 1890s the wooden building comprising a waiting room and toilets was added. Although it is still daylight, the oil lamps on the platform are actually lit! (Beamish Museum)

47. We can now enjoy a better view of the mass of roses over the station house entrance. The wooden building was for passengers, the two-storey addition on the right is extra accommodation. Despite serving a community of only 570 people the station remained staffed until 1966. It is still in residential use. (K.Hoole Collection)

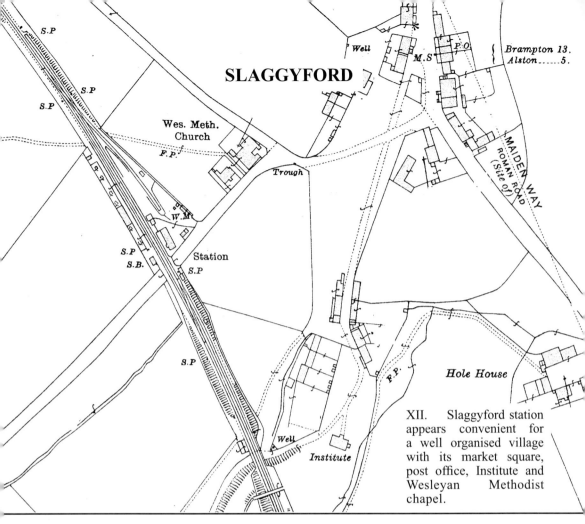

SLAGGYFORD

Brampton 13.
Alston ... 5.

Wes. Meth.
Church

Trough

Station

Hole House

Institute

Well

XII. Slaggyford station appears convenient for a well organised village with its market square, post office, Institute and Wesleyan Methodist chapel.

48.   The stationmaster's house was on the other side of the line from the platform with its 1890 wooden shed. The loop was 242 yards long. The photographer is in the rear, not in the front of the DMU, as the gentleman runs across the track. (Stations UK)

49.   In this winter scene we observe that the signal box has gone and the train is required to stop before crossing the road. The trees behind the waiting room have grown. The station house is now a private house. (K.Hoole Collection)

50.   This view of the station is from the level crossing. On the right is Hawthorn Leslie 0-4-0ST no.3732 of 1928, bought from Dunston Power Station in the initial attempts to preserve the branch. The date is 19th May 1974. (R.R.Darsley)

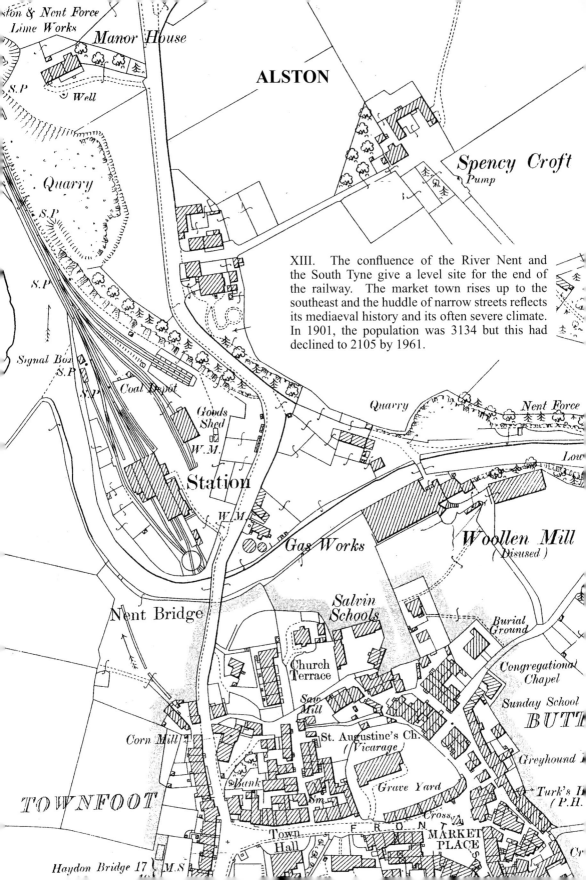

ston & Nent Force
Lime Works

Manor House

ALSTON

S.P

Well

Quarry

S.P

Spency Croft

Pump

S.P

Signal Box

S.P

Coal Depot

XIII.   The confluence of the River Nent and
the South Tyne give a level site for the end of
the railway.   The market town rises up to the
southeast and the huddle of narrow streets reflects
its mediaeval history and its often severe climate.
In 1901, the population was 3134 but this had
declined to 2105 by 1961.

Quarry

Nent Force

Low

Goods
Shed

W.M.

Station

W.M.

Gas Works

Woollen Mill
(Disused)

Nent Bridge

*Salvin
Schools*

Burial
Ground

Church
Terrace

*Congregational
Chapel*

Saw
Mill

Sunday School

BUTT

Corn Mill

St. Augustine's Ch.
(Vicarage

Greyhound

TOWNFOOT

Bank

Sm

Grave Yard

Turk's
(P.H

Town
Hall

F R O N T

Cross

**MARKET
PLACE**

Haydon Bridge 17   M.S.

51.   The terminus at Alston is here viewed from the hill behind the gasworks. On the left is the station with its train shed. The goods shed is behind the gasworks chimney and the coal staithes were on the right. (K.Hoole Collection)

52.   The station is seen from the approach road. The style of the imposing building is similar to that of the Newcastle & Berwick Railway. The site of the goods yard with its 3-ton crane is now a small industrial estate. (K.Hoole Collection)

53.　The goods yard in more prosperous days had livestock pens, a healthy van traffic in the goods dock and the coal staithes, the buffers of which are just showing to the right of the shed. Alston could handle lime and ore as well as coal. (K.Hoole Collection)

54.　The goods shed is viewed from the north and a drop-side wagon is on the siding that led under the road to the gasworks.　Good services ceased on 6th September 1965. (K.Hoole Collection)

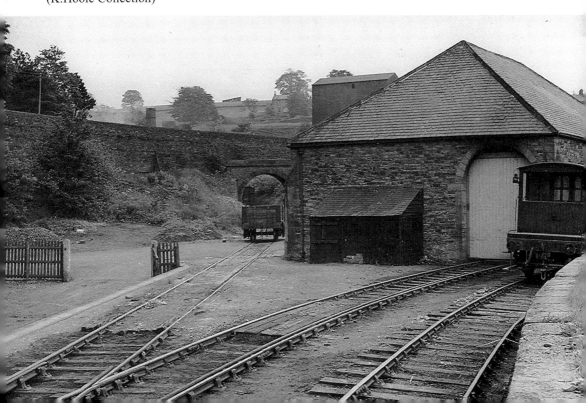

55.　　　Here Alston station is at its busiest. Class G5 0-4-4T no.67315 is at the passenger platform and class J39 0-6-0 no.64851 is in the shed. The tracks to the turntable have been barred, as the turntable was disused by 1951. There is an interesting old NER carriage in the shadow of the train shed on 12th April 1952. (J.W.Armstrong Trust)

56.	Decay set in during the 1960s. The engine shed closed and the track was gradually removed. The overall roof was dismantled, though here it has only lost the rotting wooden screens. A class 101 DMU is waiting to depart for Haltwhistle. (K.Hoole Collection)

57.	British Railways passenger services ceased on 3rd May 1976, but the station reopened in 1983 as the headquarters of the South Tyneside Railway which operates a 2-foot gauge railway north towards Slaggyford. It was photographed on 28th January 2005. (R.R.Darsley)

58.	*Helen Kathryn,* an 0-4-0WT built by Henschel as no. 28035 in 1948, leaves the station on a South Tynedale Railway train on 26th September 1998. (R.R.Darsley)

59.   These are the new carriage sheds and the approach to the station with the South Tynedale Railway carriage sidings ground frame in the small building on the left. The date is 28th January 2005. (R.R.Darsley)

60.   We retrace our route northwards. The South Tynedale Railway train is waiting at Gilderdale on 19th June 1988 to leave for Alston. It is one of a series of special trains to celebrate the Newcastle and Carlisle Railway's 150th year. No.6 0-4-0WTT, Henschel no.16047 of 1918, is named *Thomas Edmondson* after the NCR employee who invented the card ticket. (I.S.Carr)

61.   The terminus of the line in 2006 was Kirkhaugh. In the Summer of 2005, Polish 0-6-0WTT no. 10 *Naklo* (Chrzanow no. 3459 of 1957) waits with its train to return to Alston. (M.H.Smith)

3. Over the Summit
BLENKINSOPP HALL HALT

62.   Blenkinsopp Hall Halt was a private station for the Hall. The single-storey lodge with its fine finials was also the station building, but the halt was out of use by 1875. (R.R.Darsley)

63.   Blenkinsopp signal box guarded an important crossing of the railway with the A69. Children watch class A4 4-6-2 no.4498 *Sir Nigel Gresley* rush past on 'The Tynesider' excursion on 6th October 1973. The crossing is out of use now, as the A69 bypass diverted the road traffic. (T.Heavyside)

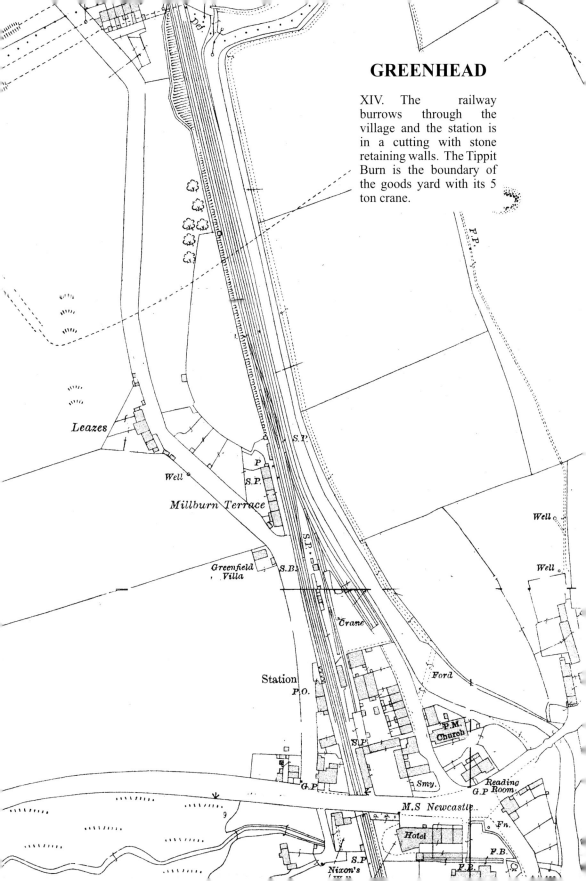

GREENHEAD

XIV. The railway burrows through the village and the station is in a cutting with stone retaining walls. The Tippit Burn is the boundary of the goods yard with its 5 ton crane.

Leazes

Well

Millburn Terrace

S.P.

P
S.P.

Greenfield Villa

S.B.

S.P.

Well

Well

Crane

Ford

Station
P.O.

P.M. Church

S.P.

Smy.

Reading G.P Room

G.P.

M.S Newcastle

Fn.

9

Hotel

F.B.

S.P.
Nixon's

F.B.

64.   This is a view of the station looking west from the overbridge. The platforms with their wooden shelters were separate from the original NCR station which is to the right hand side. The large building behind the down platform is a group of cottages entered from the road at first floor level. This is 1967, the year of closure. (Stations UK)

65.   Through the foliage on 30th June 2003 is the original NCR station and the site of the goods yard, still used as a coal depot with many of its original features and buildings. The station building has been heavily modified with a flat-roofed extension at the rear, but the former engine shed is probably one of the oldest examples left in the UK. (R.R.Darsley)

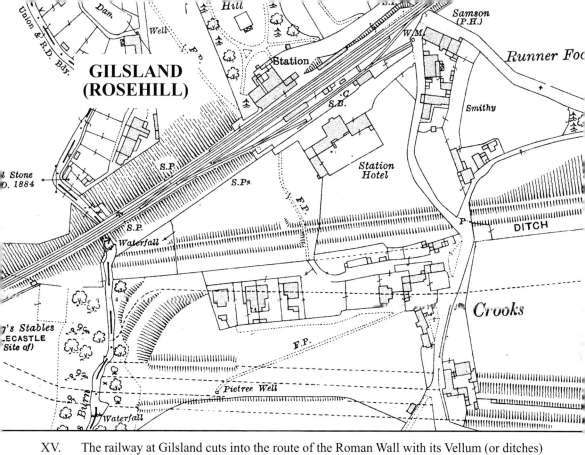

XV.   The railway at Gilsland cuts into the route of the Roman Wall with its Vellum (or ditches) and mile-castles. This would not be the first desecration of the 2000 year old construction. Most of the old farmhouses are built with the small dressed Roman stones.

66.   Rosehill served a spa, which later became a convalescent home, and the very elegant station reflected that with its extra buildings and glass screens. This 1858 photograph shows how the NCR graded the station forecourt across the tracks. (Carlisle Library)

67.   It appears that the running tracks were lowered to allow the provision of platforms, as the proportions of the building and canopy remain the same. The stationmaster poses with his staff. There is a cordon fruit tree growing up the wall under the glass. The station was named Gilsland in 1869. (Carlisle Library)

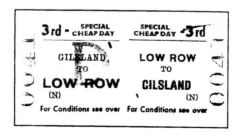

68.   In 1902 the glass canopy was replaced by a hideous iron shelter, later roofed with corrugated iron. On the down platform was a signal box and a stone waiting shed with a wood and glass front built by the NER. (Carlisle Library)

69.   This view shows the buildings on the down platform more clearly. On the up platform, the iron shelter has gone except for the pillars on which oil lamps were hung at night. The disfiguring dormer windows in the roof were not a 1960s addition as might be thought. They were added in 1910! This picture is 1967, the year of passenger service withdrawal. (Stations UK)

70.   Denton Village is a small crossing with a ground frame. There is also a fine house that faces and has access to the railway but has never been a station. Despite being the highest part of the line, the railway is level for six miles between Gilsland and Brampton. The date is 30th June 2003. (R.R.Darsley)

2nd - SINGLE   SINGLE - 2nd

Low Row to

Low Row   Low Row
Gilsiand   Gilsiand

GILSLAND

(N)   0/8   Fare   0/8   (N)

For conditions see over For conditions see over

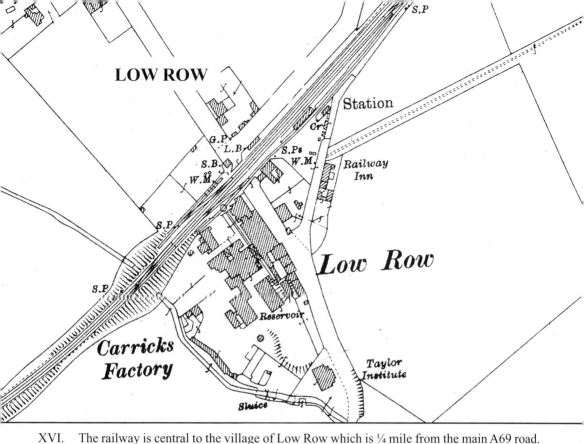

LOW ROW

Station

G.P.
L.B.
S.B.
W.M.
S.Ps
W.M.
Railway
Inn

S.P.

S.P.

Low Row

Carricks Factory

Reservoir

Taylor
Institute

Sluice

XVI. The railway is central to the village of Low Row which is ¼ mile from the main A69 road. Sidings served the Naworth Coal Company and Carrick's Creamery. A wagon turntable enabled wagons to be placed right inside the creamery.

71. This was never a busy station and passenger services were withdrawn on 1st January 1959. Goods services lasted longer until 5th April 1965. After passenger services ceased, the platforms gradually disappeared. This is the 1836 station house, still occupied in 2005. The NER installed wooden buildings on both platforms. (R.R.Darsley)

72.   The tall NER signal box still controls the level crossing. The gates close across the railway only on the west side. (R.R.Darsley)

NAWORTH

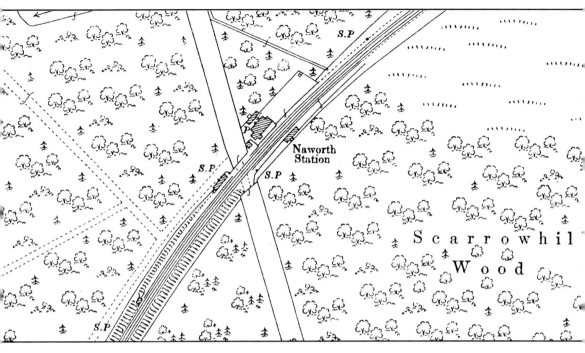

XVII. The Earl of Carlisle had a private station for his home, Naworth Castle, set deep in woodland on the estate. There were no goods facilities.

73.   Here the single-storey station house is opposite the down platform with its wooden building. The up platform had this unusual dip in it for the road crossing. (K.Hoole Collection)

74.   The station opened to the public in 1871. The stationmaster and his family are outside the station house. The rather fine down platform waiting room is for the excursion traffic to Naworth Castle. (K.Hoole Collection)

75.   The station house had a second storey added in an attractive way. When the station closed in 1952, the platforms and wooden buildings were rapidly removed. In 1967 the station was boarded up but in 2005, it was back in use as a private house. (Stations UK)

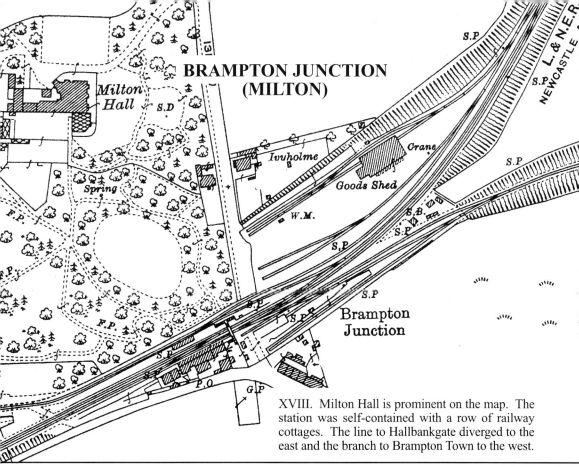

BRAMPTON JUNCTION
(MILTON)

XVIII. Milton Hall is prominent on the map. The station was self-contained with a row of railway cottages. The line to Hallbankgate diverged to the east and the branch to Brampton Town to the west.

76.   Milton station was renamed Brampton Junction in 1870. It was renamed Brampton in 1971, 48 years after the Brampton Town line closed. The 1836 building can be identified in the centre of the long structure that was on the down platform. At the far end are two small cottages. These were incorporated in the 1883 extensions either side of the original station house. The platform has been built up to the sill level of the house and cottages. (K.Hoole Collection)

77.   Here class B1 4-6-0 no.61276 heads an up train through the station, believed to be a summer Saturday working from Glasgow to Scarborough – note the LMSR coaches. (J.W.Armstrong Trust)

78.   This view is from the footbridge. The line to Newcastle is to the left with a large goods yard to the north. The line to the right of the signal box is the Earl of Carlisle's Railway to Kirkhouse and Lambley. Originally a siding came along the fence into a bay platform. (K.Hoole Collection)

79.   We are looking west in June 2003. The buildings on the down platform have gone, being replaced by a bus shelter. No.142024 is in front of the NER wooden waiting room that has been heavily altered. This up platform was originally an island platform with the train from Brampton Town arriving between the waiting-room and the trees of Milton Hall Park. The distant semaphore behind the bridge was a new replacement in 2003. (R.R.Darsley)

BRAMPTON TOWN

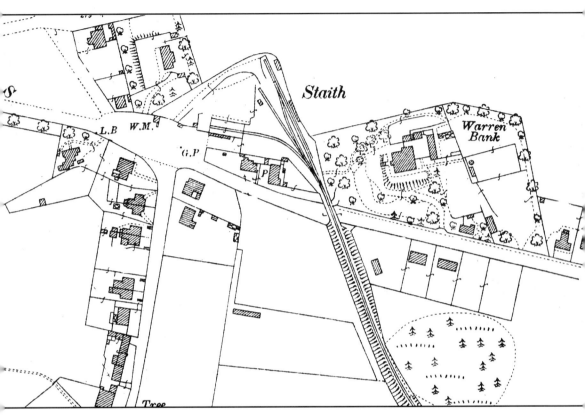

XIX.   Brampton Town does not warrant the name station, though the mapmaker in 1921 may not have been sure if the passenger service was still running, but the station buildings are shown. The staith proper is the most westerly siding.

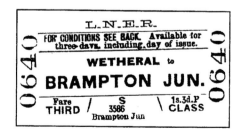

80.　This is one of the horse-drawn 'Dandy' wagons photographed at Kirkhouse where the Earl of Carlisle's railway offices and works were situated.　By 1835, passengers were carried from Midgeholme to Brampton on market days at a fare of one shilling.　After the opening of the realigned line in 1836, six days before the NCR, there was a daily 'Dandy' service from Milton to Brampton Town. (K.Hoole Collection)

81.　Persistent complaints about the 'Dandy' service led Thompson in 1881 to purchase three ex-London & North Western Railway carriages and a new 0-4-0T *Dandie Dinmont* Neilson no.2738 of 1881. (K.Hoole Collection)

82.　　The branch was reopened by the NER in 1913. Here the opening passenger train is in the branch bay platform at Brampton Junction on 1st August. The locomotive is a NER class BTP 0-4-4T between two auto coaches and everyone is dressed for the occasion awaiting the VIPs. (K.Hoole Collection)

83.　　The VIPs have arrived! The special train is on the down platform at Brampton Junction with the official NER party and the NER inspection saloon. The ladies' hats are most impressive! (K.Hoole Collection)

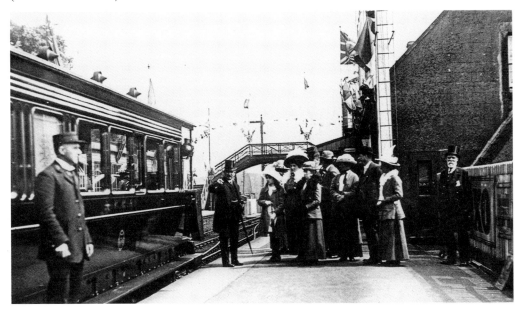

84.   The original 1836 skew arch bridge in Brampton took the railway over the road. It was replaced in 1912 by a less attractive girder bridge, which was dismantled in 1924. The trackbed from Brampton Junction is now a footpath which ends with steps from the bridge abutment down to the road. (K.Hoole Collection)

85.   Brampton Town had a short platform with the wooden building providing an office and a waiting room. NER class BTP 0-4-4T no.1089 has a one-coach train. The track work shows the engine release loop and one of the two goods sidings. The population census showed that Brampton grew from 2,500 at the turn of the century, to 3,500 60 years later. It might have grown further had it been on a direct line to Carlisle. (K.Hoole Collection)

4. Brampton to Lambley
KIRKHOUSE

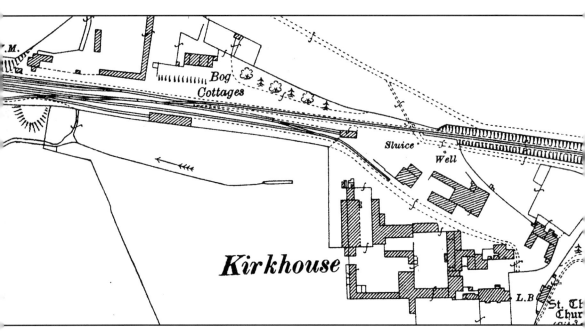

XX.   The offices and works of the Earl of Carlisle's Railway were at Kirkhouse. Here also were the assembly sidings where full wagons were marshalled into trains and empty wagons sent back up the incline to Hallbankgate.

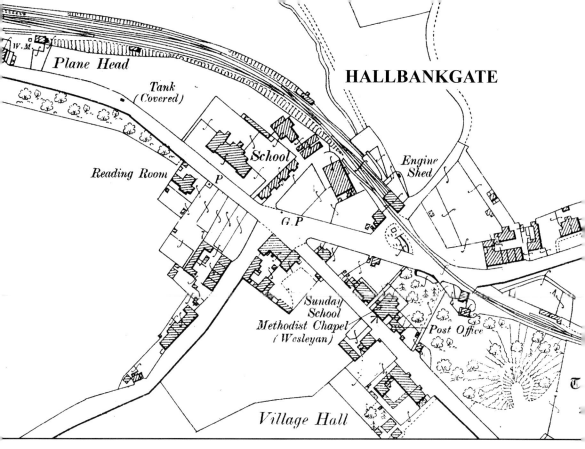

XXI.   From Kirkhouse to Hallbankgate, the line included a rope incline that had a shared centre-rail with a 'meeting' or passing loop midway. The three rail top section can be seen on the western edge of the map.

86.   The incline was a balanced working, the gravity of full loads descending hauling up the empty rakes. This photograph, taken in 1952, shows the incline control cabin at Planehead, near the summit at Hallbankgate. (J.W.Armstrong Trust)

87.   This is Hallbankgate shed in 1952. While only a wagon is visible in the shed, a locomotive is in the siding on the right. The main line to Tindale, Midgeholme, Halton Lea Gate and Lambley curves in front of the attractive lodge. Shortly after Hallbankgate the main branches to Talkin and Turnhouse collieries climb away to the south. (J.W.Armstrong Trust)

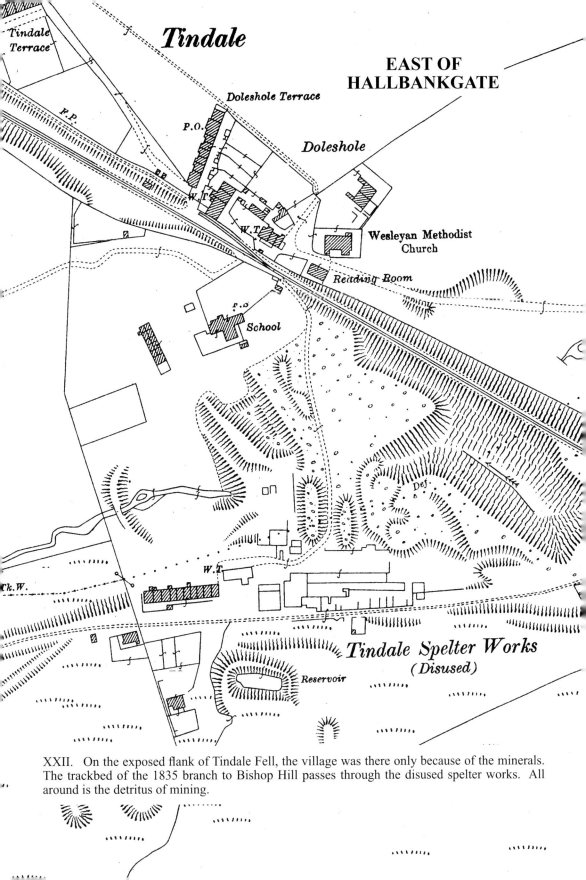

Tindale Terrace

Tindale

F.P.

Doleshole Terrace

P.O.

Doleshole

W.T

W.T

Wesleyan Methodist
Church

Reading Room

F.S

School

Dej.

W.T

k.W.

Tindale Spelter Works
(Disused)

Reservoir

XXII. On the exposed flank of Tindale Fell, the village was there only because of the minerals.
The trackbed of the 1835 branch to Bishop Hill passes through the disused spelter works. All
around is the detritus of mining.

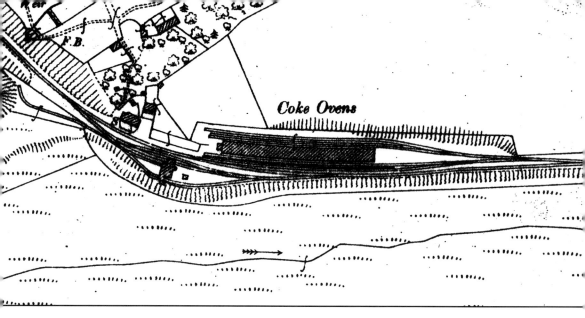

XXIII. As the line proceeds east at an altitude of 800-900 feet, it served the coke ovens and colliery at Midgeholme.

88.   An impression of a scene at Halton Lea Gate depot in about 1840 was drawn by S.Barnes. The locomotives are *Rocket* 0-2-2OC from the Liverpool and Manchester Railway, and *Belted Will* 0-4-0VC built at Kirkhouse in 1838/9. (RCTS)

89.   The track from Midgeholme to Lambley Colliery closed in 1908 and this was then the Lambley Fell rail head. The branch closed on 2nd May 1960. (K.Hoole Collection)

XXIV. Lambley Colliery is where the Earl of Carlisle's Railway met the Lambley branch of the Alston line. For over 50 years the collieries had the ability to send coal either way, which was a valuable asset especially in winter.

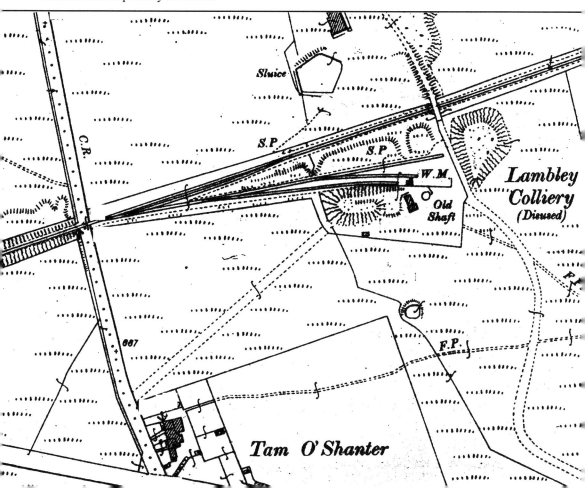

5. Brampton Fell to Carlisle
BRAMPTON FELL

90.   The NCR single-storey building with its huge chimney stack was a passenger station from 1836 until 1850. It is still in use as a private house. The signal box is the other side of the crossing. This is the closest point to the Talkin Tarn beauty spot. (R.R.Darsley)

91.   Gelt viaduct is a three-arch red sandstone structure crossing at 64ft above the river at an angle of 63°. Each span was 30ft and, when built, it was the largest of its kind. To the east, and difficult for photographers to reach, was Hell Beck cutting (40ft deep and ¼ mile long) and embankment (73ft high at its maximum). To the west was the famous Cowran cutting. (R.R.Darsley)

WEST OF BRAMPTON FELL

92.   Class B1 4-6-0 no. 61238 *Leslie Runciman* is seen in Cowran Cutting with a Carlisle-Newcastle freight on 12th April 1958. The hand dug cutting was a mile long with a maximum depth retaining wall of 110ft x 14ft high. Cowran Cutting, when it was built, was the largest in the country. (R.Leslie)

93.   Co-CoDE no.66135 is on a Shap to Lackenby limestone train on 19th August 2003. Cowran cutting is still impressive, even today. (P.J.Robinson)

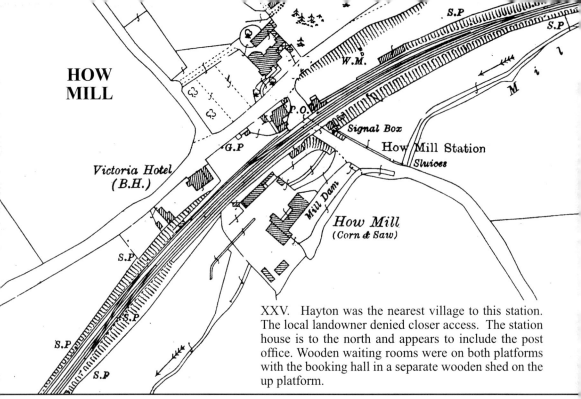

HOW MILL

Victoria Hotel
(B.H.)

How Mill
(Corn & Saw)

Signal Box

How Mill Station
Sluices

XXV. Hayton was the nearest village to this station. The local landowner denied closer access. The station house is to the north and appears to include the post office. Wooden waiting rooms were on both platforms with the booking hall in a separate wooden shed on the up platform.

94. The platforms were staggered across the level crossing, the up to the east and the down to the west. Here class Q6 0-8-0 no.63441 passes through the station with a Blaydon to Carlisle freight train on 12th January 1957. (R.Leslie)

95.   The large station house exists as a private accommodation on the up side west of the level crossing. A NER signal box stood on the down side east of the crossing. Passenger and goods services ended in 1959 and the platforms were soon removed. (R.R.Darsley)

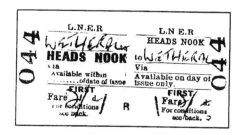

HEADS NOOK

XXVI. The station buildings are to the west of the overbridge with the goods sidings to the east of it. Catchpoints prevent any runaway wagons from fouling the up line in the cutting.

96. Class B1 4-6-0 no.61100 on the Stranraer to Newcastle train passes through Heads Nook on 23rd July 1960. The gardens are well maintained and a NER serpent seat is on the up platform. (P.J.Robinson)

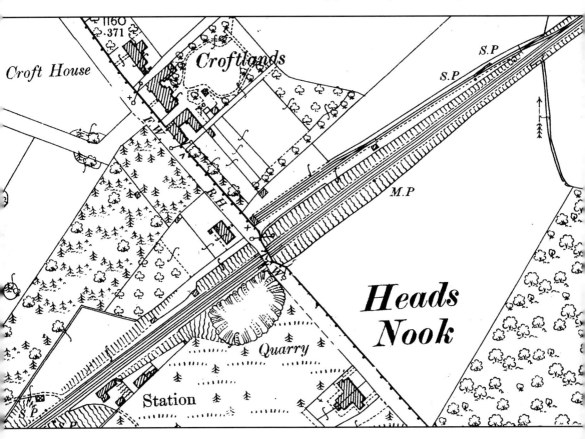

97. The station opened in 1862. The plain station house, above the down platform, is still in use as a private dwelling. The down platform had a stone and timber building with a pent roof. The up platform had a pitch roofed timber building. Goods services ceased in 1965 and passenger services in 1967, when the photograph was taken. (Stations UK)

WEST OF HEADS NOOK

98.   There were no freight facilities at Heads Nook, but half a mile west was a siding at Broadwath Crossing. Here class K1 2-6-0 no.62029 passes Broadwath with a Blaydon to Carlisle freight on 1st January 1957. (R.Leslie)

99.   A dirty class B1 4-6-0 passes Corby Gates signal box prior to crossing Wetheral Viaduct. The coaches are still on Corby Viaduct. This crosses Corby Burn with seven sandstone arches of 40ft span and total length of 480ft. At its highest point it is 70ft above the burn. The viaduct is now surrounded by trees. (K.Hoole Collection)

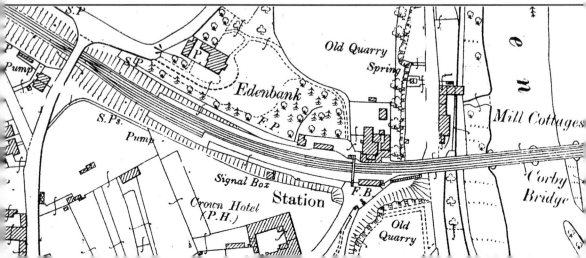

100. The main goods facilities for Wetheral were at Corby Gates and they closed in April 1955. There is a footpath across the north side of Wetheral viaduct which at one time cost a half-penny toll unless you were going to church or choir practice in Wetheral. (K.Hoole Collection)

101. Class K1 2-6-0 no.62030 crosses Wetheral Viaduct on 16th August 1952 with a coal train heading for Carlisle. The viaduct is 564ft long with five arches of 80ft and a height of 95ft above the River Eden. (J.W.Armstrong Trust)

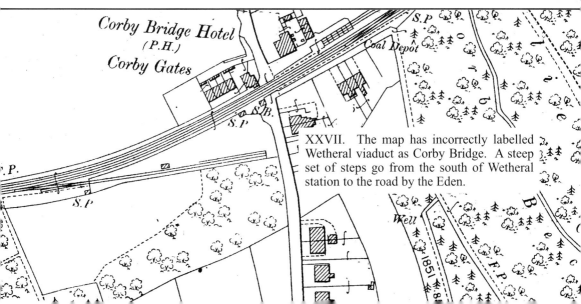

XXVII. The map has incorrectly labelled Wetheral viaduct as Corby Bridge. A steep set of steps go from the south of Wetheral station to the road by the Eden.

WETHERAL

102.　　The station in NCR days had a full canopy over the single-storey buildings on the up side at the west end of the viaduct.　Part of the delicate canopy survived the closure of the station in 1967 to be there when it reopened in 1981. The village grew from 3,293 in 1901 to 3,852 in 1961. It has continued to grow, giving support to the reopening. (Carlisle Library)

103.　　The up platform had another single-storey building plus a brick and timber waiting room, shown here as class B1 4-6-0 no.61100 comes through the station.　The down platform also had a waiting room.　The signal box was on the cutting side (left) above the down platform. The goods dock and a 5-ton crane can be seen at the end of the platform. (R.Leslie)

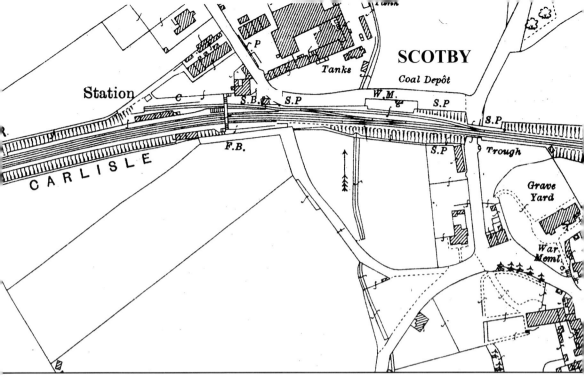

XXVIII. Scotby had two stations with the village in between. The station to the south was on the Settle & Carlisle Railway. Prominent in the NCR station layout are the coal depot and the large footbridge, both platforms and the approach roads.

104.   The NCR shelter on the down platform had the booking office in one corner. It was replaced in 1889. On the up platform, the NER built a standard wooden structure. A class J39 0-6-0 enters the station with a coal train. The footbridge to the left led to the north entrance and the stationmaster's house. (Stations UK)

105.   The red sandstone station house is all that is left of the station which survived until 1959, closing to goods and passengers at the same time. The other station was a typical Midland Railway rural station and closed in 1942, but is still a private house. Bus competition was the cause of both closures, though with the growth of the village there might be a case for reopening one. (R.R.Darsley)

WEST OF SCOTBY

106.   Approaching Carlisle from the east, Durranhill was a mass of sidings leading to a junction with the Settle & Carlisle. This view is from the road bridge to Harraby in May 1959 and a class 101 DMU is on its way from Carlisle to Newcastle. In the distance on the left behind NER Durranhill Junction signal box are the Midland Railway sidings. To the right are the NER sidings and the beginnings of a new industrial estate. (R.Leslie)

CARLISLE LONDON ROAD

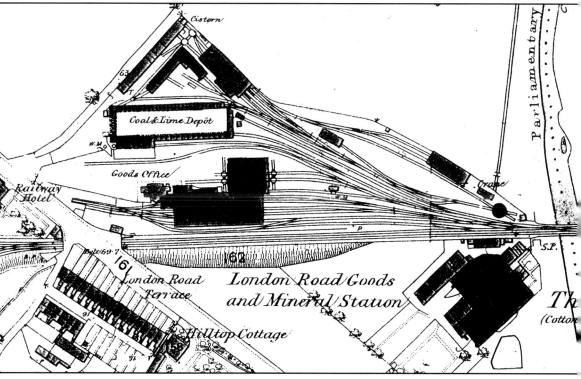

XXIX. This first edition Ordnance Survey map shows the NCR station as a goods station though the overall passenger station roof is still in position between the ticket office (Goods Office) and the original goods shed.

107.   Carlisle London Road was not the planned terminus, for the line continued to the Canal Basin, but it was considered to be more convenient for passengers, as it was situated on the main south road of the city. This is J.W.Carmichael's sketch from 1835. (Tullie Museum, Carlisle)

108.   This is the rear view of the original station in 1881. In 1863, the NER had obtained entry to Carlisle Citadel Station and the depot remained for goods traffic only. The goods sheds are also the original NCR buildings. This photograph appears to be an official one, taken just before the new goods depot was built, which greatly modified these buildings. (Carlisle Library)

109.   The NER built a large locomotive depot at London Road to the north of the station/goods shed and warehouse. It had two turntables under the pitched roof, an elevated coaling stage and repair facilities. It closed in 1933 but remains as a road haulage warehouse.
(K.Hoole Collection)

110. This is the interior of Carlisle London Road engine shed on 4th May 1933, just before closure. The locomotive is class J24 0-6-0 no.1944, one of those transferred to the shed in 1927. When London Road closed, this locomotive remained in Carlisle Canal Bank shed until withdrawn in 1938. The locomotive on the other turntable sidings appears to be one of Reid's NBR class C (J36) 0-6-0s. (K.Hoole Collection)

111. Cowans Sheldon & Co Ltd's St Nicholas Works was the last large industrial enterprise before entering Carlisle Citadel Station. In the distance a NER class 398 0-6-0 is shunting two wagons. No.991 of this class from Carlisle was earmarked for preservation, but Great Northern Railway 4-2-2 no. 1 was saved instead. (Carlisle Library)

112. Cowans Sheldon & Co Ltd built all types of cranes, railway turntables and the occasional tram type locomotive, but are famous for their railway breakdown cranes which sold all over the world. Here is one of their official photographs of a steam crane for the Jamaican Government Railway on test at Carlisle. (Beamish Museum)

EAST OF CARLISLE

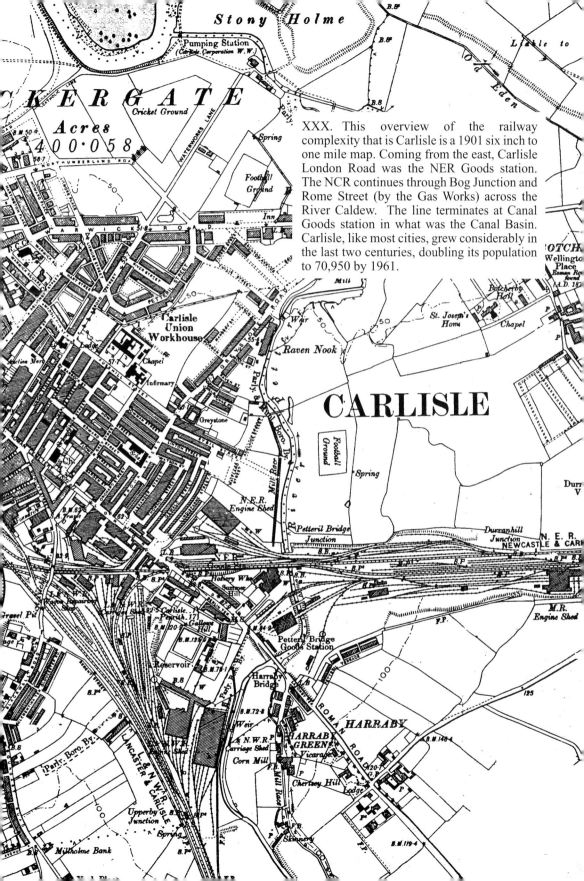

XXX. This overview of the railway complexity that is Carlisle is a 1901 six inch to one mile map. Coming from the east, Carlisle London Road was the NER Goods station. The NCR continues through Bog Junction and Rome Street (by the Gas Works) across the River Caldew. The line terminates at Canal Goods station in what was the Canal Basin. Carlisle, like most cities, grew considerably in the last two centuries, doubling its population to 70,950 by 1961.

113.   We are looking from the south end of Carlisle Citadel station on 25th September 1999. No. 56029 is taking the 1864 curve to London Road and the Newcastle line. The West Coast main line rises over the NCR connection to the Maryport and Carlisle Railway, which in the early days used Carlisle London Road station until it opened its own station at Crown Street. A class 142 DMU from Maryport on the MCR link approaches Citadel Station. (R.R.Darsley)

(top right) 114.The front elevation of the station is shown from William Tite's original plans of 1846. With a few modifications, the main facade was completed in late 1848 though the clock was not added until 1853. The station was opened in 1847, although the NER did not get access until 1863, but the NCR never got in! (Carlisle Library)

(right) 115.We look inside the train shed of Carlisle Citadel station in the late 1920s. No.1 and No.2 Bay platforms have always been the NER Newcastle platforms and a class D17/2 4-4-0 is in No.1 Bay. These locomotives had a clerestory on the cab roof and eight of the class were shedded at Carlisle London Road between 1923 and 1931. (M.M.Earley/National Railway Museum)

CARLISLE CITADEL

FRONT ELEVATION
Of the General Station, Court Square, Carlisle.—Mr. Tite Architect.

116.   The huge overall glass roof was badly neglected during the war and work began in 1954 to cut back the roof from the main line platform 1 and at both ends where it was replaced by a low level canopy. Here class 4MT 2-6-4T no.80080 on the 12.30 for Kirkby Stephen and no.156448 on the 13.28 to Middlesbrough via Newcastle wait to depart on 12th March 1993. (T.Heavyside)

117.   No.142065 is in the Newcastle platform on 21st June 2003. Behind are the hangings for the 150th Anniversary of Carlisle Citadel in 1997. The left hand three show the north of the station in steam days, and the right hand three, the Viaduct Goods yard behind the station. (R.R.Darsley)

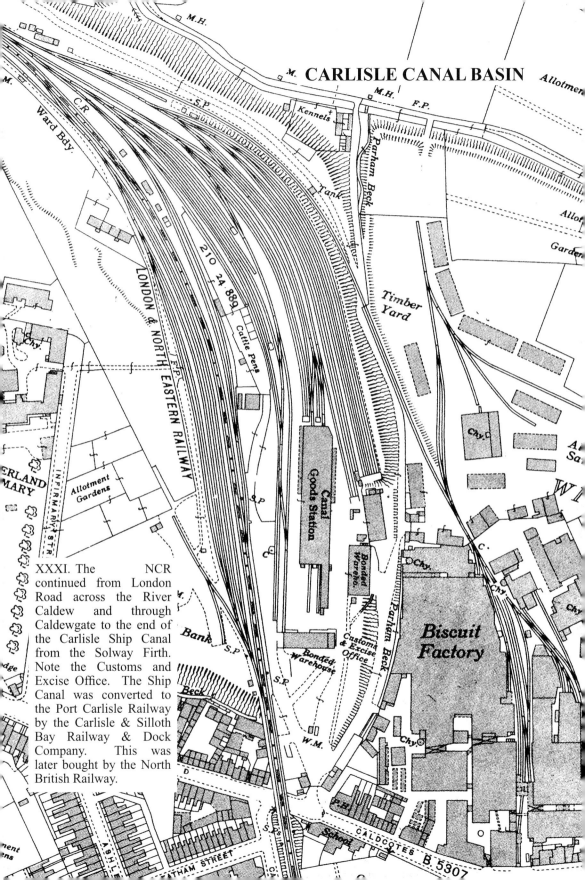

CARLISLE CANAL BASIN

XXXI. The NCR continued from London Road across the River Caldew and through Caldewgate to the end of the Carlisle Ship Canal from the Solway Firth. Note the Customs and Excise Office. The Ship Canal was converted to the Port Carlisle Railway by the Carlisle & Silloth Bay Railway & Dock Company. This was later bought by the North British Railway.

118.   This is the NCR gatehouse at the Dalston Road level crossing at Murrell Hill. To the west of this crossing was a large set of staithes for coal merchants. Their remains were still visible in 2005. (K.Hoole Collection)

119.   This view was taken from the canal goods station which was built on the canal basin. Sidings from Canal Junction come back at a lower level to serve the famous Carr's Biscuit factory. One of Drummond's NBR class C (J32) 0-6-0 shunts the factory and the Alexandra Saw Mills in Willowholme. (Carlisle Library)

120.   J.W.Carmichael sketched the Canal Basin in 1835. This was the terminus of the first cross-country railway in the world. The Carlisle Ship Canal lasted from 1821 to 1853 when it was converted in eight months to the Port Carlisle Railway. A new station was then built by the Port Road overbridge. It opened on 22nd June 1854 but closed on 1st July 1864. The Basin is now the Port Road Business Park and only the gatekeeper's cottage remains. (Tullie Museum, Carlisle)

MP Middleton Press

EVOLVING THE ULTIMATE RAIL ENCYCLOPEDIA

Easebourne Lane, Midhurst, West Sussex.
GU29 9AZ   Tel:01730 813169

www.middletonpress.co.uk   email:info@middletonpress.co.uk

A-0 906520   B-1 873793   C-1 901706   D-1 904474

OOP Out of Print at time of printing - Please check current availability   **BROCHURE AVAILABLE SHOWING NEW TITLES**